Bingham William

A Letter from an American Now Resident in London

Bingham William

A Letter from an American Now Resident in London

ISBN/EAN: 9783337149956

Printed in Europe, USA, Canada, Australia, Japan

Cover: Foto ©Andreas Hilbeck / pixelio.de

More available books at **www.hansebooks.com**

À

LETTER

FROM AN

AMERICAN,

Now refident in LONDON,

TO A

MEMBER OF PARLIAMENT,

On the Subject of the

RESTRAINING PROCLAMATION;

AND CONTAINING

STRICTURES

ON

LORD SHEFFIELD's PAMPHLET,

ON THE

COMMERCE

OF THE

AMERICAN STATES.

Said to be written by WILLIAM BINGHAM, Efquire; late Agent for the Congress of the United States of America, at *Martinico*.

To which are added,

MENTOR's REPLY to PHOCION's LETTER; with fome OBSERVATIONS on TRADE, addreffed to the Citizens of NEW-YORK.

PHILADELPHIA:

PRINTED and SOLD BY ROBERT BELL, in Third-Street,

M, D C C, L X X X I V.

A

L E T T E R

F R O M   A N

A M E R I C A N,

C O N T A I N I N G

S T R I C T U R E S   O N

C O M M E R C E.

SIR,

THE feceffion of fo confiderable a part of the Britifh Empire, as now conftitutes the United States, and the general acknowledgement of their independence by the powers of Europe, muft point out a very important æra in the hiftory of mankind.

The caufes that led to this great revolution, and the operations that infured its fuccefs, will hereafter afford abundant matter for the pen of fome able hiftorian.

The immediate effects that it muft have on the Syftem of European Politics, form a very ferious fubject of prefent enquiry and contemplation ; efpecially, as nations begin to be convinced of the futility of becoming great by conqueft, and more inclined to abandon the cruel fyftem of war, in order eff ctually to enrich themfelves by purfuing the peaceful line of commerce.

The United States, ftretching through fuch a variety of climates, abounding in fuch various productions, and affording fuch a vaft field for the confumption of European manufactures, muft naturally have a very intimate and active commerce with the different States of Europe.

From adventitious circumftances, peculiarly favorable to Great Britain, no nation poffeffes opportunities of fo effectually promoting this connection ; and from her dependence on commerce, for the fupport of her power and importance, no nation is fo pointedly interefted in the improvement of thefe advantages.

She has already brought her affairs to the brink of ruin, from continuing too long a flave to impofture and delufion. It is time to recover her from her lethargy ; this perhaps may prove a diffi-

cult

cult tafk, as ignorant and interefted writers are ftill endeavouring to impofe their ill-digefted and pernicious fyftems on the public mind, and to imprefs fentiments, which, if adopted into the politics of this country, would be entirely fubverfive of a commercial connection betwixt Great Britain and the United States of America.

I fhall fubmit my opinions on this fubject, to your confideration, and have little doubt of a coincidence of fentiment.

You muft remember that after the conclufion of the war, a Bill was introduced into the Houfe of Commons, by Mr. Pitt, (then Chancellor of the Exchequer) in order to ferve as a temporary regulation for the trade of the United States. In perfect conformity with the fpirit of this Bill, it was expected a permanent connection betwixt the two Countries, would be formed by treaty ; it had in view a fyftem of liberal intercourfe, and was received in America with univerfal approbation, as the harbinger of returning affections.

Under a firm perfuafion that Great Britain would perfevere in the line of conduct, that this Bill prefcribed, the United States opened all their ports to Britifh fhipping, and received them, without any other reftrictions than thofe, which veffels belonging to their own citizens, were expofed to.

A change of miniftry foon after took place, and likewife a change of meafures ; the advocates for the American war compofed a part of it ; the effects were foon vifible : a Proclamation, virtually reftraining all intercourfe betwixt the United States and the Weft Indies, except in Britifh fhipping, made its appearance.

This meafure was in every refpect impolitic and unwife, as it was natural to imagine that it would make unfavourable impreffions in regard to the views of Great Britain, that would remain long, and affect deeply ; and would have a tendency to convince the United States that the fame fyftem of infatuated councils, that fevered the two countries afunder, ftill had an afcendency in the Britifh Cabinet, and was likely to continue an infuperable barrier to a free and unreftrained connection.

Much about the fame time Lord Sheffield publifhed a pamphlet, which was intended to juftify the prudent precaution of fuch meafures, as effentially neceffary to the future wealth and power of Great Britain ; it is faid to have had a very ferious effect on the minds of the people in England, the majority of whom, as in all countries, are more prone to receive the opinions of others, than be at the trouble of furnifhing arguments for themfelves.

However, it will not be difficult to prove, that his reafoning is extremely flimfy and fallacious ; entirely remote from the principles of commercial legiflation, and fupported on a fyftem of acknowledged error.

Previous to entering on a refutation of his doctrine, it will be neceffary to premife fome few reflections, on the advantages that

the

the West India Islands will derive, from being indulged in an intercourse with the United States, from which the adoption of Lord Sheffield's system would entirely exclude them.

The soil, the climate, and consequently the productions of the United States, are so various, that they can furnish almost every article that they can furnish almost every article that the wants and conveniences of the islands can require; and from circumstances of local situation, can supply them more abundantly, more expeditiously on better terms, and less subject to contingencies, than they can be procured from Europe; insomuch, that the West India Planters have always regarded a commercial connection with the United States as essential to the well-being and improvement of the islands, and have deprecated the loss of it, as a most fatal blow to their flourishing existence.

The articles which the Colonist indispensably stands in need of, are flour, biscuit, Indian corn, rice, beans, peas, potatoes, salt beef, pork, cheese, butter, beer, cod and other kinds of salt fish, whale oil, candles, tallow, soap, tobacco, naval stores, horses, poultry, live cattle, bar iron, building wood of all kinds, frames of houses, masts, spars, hogshead staves, heading, shingles, plank both pine and oak, &c.

The United States can, not only abundantly, and at all times, supply these articles, but can furnish them on far more moderate terms, than they can be imported from Europe.

Experience has proved, that no food is so cheap and nourishing to the slaves as Indian corn, of which there must necessarily be a regular and frequent supply, as it will not keep but a short time, exposed to the extreme warmth of the climate. Small vessels are generally employed in furnishing these supplies, as well as live stock and other articles of provisions, which could not afford to navigate with cargoes of such little value if it was not for the quickness of the voyage, and the certainty of a return freight of West India produce. These are not objects of sufficient importance for European vessels; for large quantities would frequently overstock the market, and consequently be exposed to perish in the hands of the importer.

But there are particular times when the dependence of the West Indies on the United States, is more pointedly observable. After a hurricane, that awful and tremendous convulsion of nature, that so frequently happens in the tropical climates, that levels with the ground all the buildings and improvements of a plantation, destroys the provisions, and exhibits throughout the whole country, the wildest marks of ruin and devastation : Where is the affrighted planter to look for succour and assistance ? How is he to repair his losses, promptly and effectually ?

He must give himself up to despair, if his only reliance is on European supplies : but he feels a consolation when he considers his vicinity to America, which, though but a foster mother, acting like a natural parent, flies to his relief,

After

After thefe terrible calamities, which have threatened all the miferies of famine, he has often found, from experience, that fhe has poured in fuch abundance, as to have reduced the prices of provifions, much lower than they even were previous to his misfortunes.

The advantages which this commerce prefents are founded on the broad bafis of reciprocal interefts, and a mutual exchange of neceffary commodities.

The United States, in return for the fupplies they furnifh the iflands, will receive their productions, feveral of which, fuch as rum and molaffes, may be called the excrefcences of their exports, and without recourfe to American confumption, would be in very feeble demand for the European market.

But fhould no encouragement be given to the planter, to aid the natural vigour of the foil, by the facility with which he may procure hi- provifions; and fhould the iflands be deprived of the advantages which their local fituation affords, by having the channel through which their fupplies are to be procured, ftopped up, or confined in too narrow bounds, they will not only individually fuffer, by being often expofed to a calamitous fcarcity; but the Mother Country muft finally be fenfible of the pernicious effects of fuch reftrictions. For the body politic, like the human body, has a fenfe of feeling, in its remoteft extremities. Nothing fuffers fingly by itfelf——— there " is a confent of the parts in the fyftem of both, and the " partial evil grows into univerfal mifchief " For in an exact ratio, with the rate of provifions, and other neceffaries of life will the demand for labour keep pace, and the price of Weft India produce, and its relative quantity, will rife or fall by thefe proportions, The planter confequently cannot afford his productions fo low, as to be placed in competition with the French at a foreign market, except he procures his neceffaries on the beft of terms.

On the contrary, fhould the iflands flourifh under a State of eafe and plenty, the Mother Country will be proportionably benefited; for it is an invariable rule in commercial polity, that riches always centre in the Metropolis: their diffufive influence may be compared to the circulation of the blood, which is difperfed over the whole fyftem, but always returns back to the heart, the feat of life, and is only fent back by new pulfations.

Should therefore this monopolizing fpirit which is a mockery on the induftry of a country, give way to more liberal ideas, the active ftimulus of the planter will no longer be depreffed. By being furnifhed with neceffaries on more moderate and eafy terms, he will employ lefs of his revenue, to defray the expences of his eftate; he will confequently have a refidue left to appropriate to the the extenfion of his fettlements, clearing and breaking up new grounds, which when brought into culture, will furnifh additional quantities of produce, to fupply the increafing demand.

In the courfe of attaining thefe profits to the planter, the State will greatly benefit in an increafe of her revenues, by the duties

laid

laid on the surplus quantity of produce: by the employment of a more extensive commerce and navigation, which must keep pace with the improving condition of her islands: and by fixing the balance of trade in her favour in proportion to the augmentation of her exports.

Another advantage of conspicuous character offers itself; which is their increasing consumption of manufactures, which improving establishments naturally occasion; and an increase of manufactures is always accompanied by a proportional increase of population.

Moulded by habit to a particular mode of thinking in regard to the commercial legislation of the islands, I know it will be difficult, and will require every effort of found reasoning, to break through the system of prohibitory laws, established by the British Government. But, when an increase of population and of revenue, progressive opulence and strength, are to be derived from the effects of abandoning this jealous self-obstructing policy; it is to be expected that the spirit of such contracted establishments will not be inveterate, and on mature consideration, will no longer be adhered to.

But it is asserted by Lord Sheffield, that regular supplies of provisions and necessaries may, with proper encouragement, be obtained from the remainder of the British Colonies on the continent.

These visionary suggestions are almost too ludicrous to be combated, and seem intended as a political artifice, to blind the eyes of the too credulous people, and deceive them into a belief, that their remaining territories in America are of considerable value.

It is well known, that the intenseness of the climate of Canada, with the difficulty of its navigation will scarcely admit of more than one voyage in the year to the West Indies, which require a regular and continued supply of provisions.

As for the inhospitable regions of Nova Scotia, it will be matter of wonder, and a solace to humanity, if by the unceasing industry of its inhabitants, it will be able to produce a sufficiency, for their sustenance and support.

The United States must therefore continue to be, what they always have been, the granary of the British West Indies; and if direct importations into them are not admitted of, recourse will be had to indirect supplies, through the medium of the neutral islands. All the additional expence of this circuitous route, incurred for charges of double insurance, freight, commission, &c. will fall on the Colonist, as the consumer, without very materially injuring the American merchant, who will naturally insure to himself a saving profit on his exports.

Besides, the British Government must establish a number of guarda cottas, well armed and appointed, to prevent the clandestine trade that will immediately commence betwixt the United States and their islands. A trade, that will find a support and protection, in every planter of the country, whose interest will be so immediately connected with its encouragement, will not easily be suppressed.

Even

Even under the vigorous authority of military government in the French West Indies, not all the weight of power, exerted for the purpose, could formerly prevent this species of traffic ; much less can it be expected to succeed, where the reigns of government are relatively so relaxed, as in the hands of the British Governors.

Besides, Great Britain has learned, by fatal dear-bought experience, impressed in such strong characters, as not to be soon and easily effaced, that " the true art of governing is not to govern " too much ;" and how difficult it is to rule a people by laws, that it is their interest to resist, and render nugatory.

But to counteract the force of the foregoing observations, it is asserted by Lord Sheffield, and what is much more strange, that people are so infatuated as to believe, that notwithstanding the absolute prohibition on the part of Great Britain, of admission of American vessels into her islands, still that the United States will open their ports to British shipping, and freely indulge them with the liberty of carrying off their produce.

But he must have a poor opinion of the force of his own arguments, which he has so abundantly furnished to Great Britain, in favour of this selfish system of monopolizing the carrying trade, if he does not believe, that they will operate so effectually on the minds of the Americans, as to induce them, deprived of an equalization of privilege, to adopt the same plan ; admitting that their sagacious clear-sighted politicians had not already discovered them.

His premises therefore are not admissible — the idea they convey is an insult on common sense.

I expected, that in forming an estimate of the American character, the English had been fully persuaded, from a view of the progress of their political affairs, that they were conducted by a people who seldom have so widely wandered from their interests.

Habituated to the resistance of every oppressive measure, more vigilant over their national concerns, more intent on connecting the science of politics, with the elements of commerce, as forming the most important object of the statesman's attention —— than perhaps any other nation existing, is it to be expected, they will acquiesce in a system, so derogatory to the honour, degrading to the spirit, and injurious to the interests of a great people ?

A moment's reflection must convince every dispassionate enquirer, that our legislators are better guardians of the public concerns, than to submit to so pernicious an intercourse ; especially, when it is considered, that they are selected from those, who are the best versed in the interests of the States, as relative to those of other commercial powers, and who will embrace every advantage that nature has given, or art can procure, to the improvement thereof.

He may continue to cherish the delusive idea, but I will tell him in prophetic language, what will be the consequence.

The States from a sense of common danger, and common interest, will more closely unite together, and form one general

fystem

fyftem of exclufive navigation, in regard to Great Britain, eftablifhed on clear, equal and determinate principles of commercial retaliation, which will rapidly pervade the whole Union. Already has a generous competition began to take place, betwixt them, which fhall moft cheerfully adopt, and carry into effect, thofe wife and falutary meafures, recommended by the grand council of the country, in order to make their fœderal union refpectable, and the United States, as profperous in Peace, as they have been glorious in War.

I acknowledge, that fuch public fpirited arrangements will, for a time, expofe fome of the States, to temporary inconvenience and diftrefs ; but after all the facrifices they have already made, will it be furprizing that they fhould exert this felf-denying virtue ; efpeci as it will eventually become one of the greateft fources of their future wealth and importance.

Such prohibitions, therefore, on the part of Great Britain, will operate like a charm throughout the country ; they will act like a fpur on the induftry of the inhabitants, and compel them to turn their attention more immediately to the conftruction of fhips, and the increafe of their feamen. The eaftern and middle States, which from circumftances of local fituation and character, are more peculiarly calculated for thefe purpofes, will, by vigorous exertion, by great and increafing encouragement, in a fhort time, be enabled to furnifh a fufficient fupply. Many of their trading inhabitants will be induced to refide in, and become citizens of the fouthern States, and form eftablifhments therein, in order to devote themfelves to the bufinefs of furnifhing the neceffary fhipping, for the tranfportation of their bulky produce.

Such circumftances, fortunately combining in favour of the general intereft of the republic will operate as a bond of union amongft them by occafioning their refpective citizens to continue to mix freely and intimately together.

And by making them mutually dependent on each other for reciprocal fervices, will diveft them of local attachments, and will irrefiftibly impel them to become friends, to the rights and interefts of confederated America. For as the propagation of mankind depends on the intercourfe of perfons of different fexes, fo do political connections thrive only betwixt fuch countries, as furnifh different materials for their mutual exchange, and who foon become, from a fenfe of each others wants mutually endeared to each other. Yet this fhrewd politcian infers, that the States will oppofe each other, becaufe their ftaples and their climate are dfferent—forgetting the truth of that political maxim, that intereft unites, from the fame caufe that it divides.

Therefore this felfifh arrangement which appears to predominate, in the Britifh Cabinet, and which is fuppofed to be an emanation from the fame ill fated ftar, which in your political fyftem has been fo long looked up to as your polar direction, will eventually become

B   a great a great advantage to the United States ; for I am well convinced, that they never will arrive to any eminence as a naval power, until their inhabitants are reduced to the neceffity of being the exclufive carriers of their own productions, thereby encouraging mercantile navigation, fo as to make it become a nurfery of feamen. I fay forced, for the affertion of Lord Sheffield, that our veffels navigate cheaper than thofe of Great Britain, is not founded on fact ; for when their fpeedy decay, comparatively with thofe of the Britifh, with the fcarcity of feamen, the much higher price of wages, and the neceffity of importing moft of the building materials from Europe, are taken into confideration, it will clearly be inferred, that the latter can afford their freights, at a much eafier rate.

But fhould the United States be compelled to adopt a navigation act, the profpect will then change, the demands for feamen will greatly increafe, their wages will be encouraging, and it will not be poffible to prevent their paffing into the American fervice ; for this clafs of people, as wavering and inconftant as the element that wafts them, are attached to change of climate, and are eafily allured by the profpect of greater wages, or kinder treatment.

Under the influence of the above caufes it muft be clearly evident, that the fears of our competition in the carrying trade of the Weft Indies, are entirely groundlefs. Befides, it is not probable that the Americans will feek in foreign countries for freights, when they have not perhaps above one fourth part of the neceffary fhipping to fupply their own demands, for tranfporting their produce to market : How abfurd and contradictory then are Lord Sheffield's apprehenfions ! for it is, from a prefumption of their fcarcity of fhipping, that he affirms that the Americans will not refufe their produce to the offers of Britifh veffels ; he acknowledges likewife, that the French underfel the Britifh fugars at foreign markets ; there can confequently be but little danger of the Americans being defirous of carrying them to foreign ports ; for where will be the inducement ?

In arguing againft this felfifh contracted fyftem, founded on extreme cupidity, and in favour of a free unreftrained commerce betwixt the two countries, I have no view of confulting the advantages of the United States to the exclufion of thofe of Great Britain

I know it would be folly to expect that fhe would make facrifices of her interefts, to accommodate the views of the Americans.

But it fo happens, that fhe cannot favour the United States' with an indulgence, for which they are not able to furnifh more than a reciprocal benefit.

It is expedient however to examine ftill more fully, what the grand leading argument that Lord Sheffield adduces in favour of the neceffity of totally excluding them from a participation in the Britifh Weft India trade, amounts to. He is fearful that they will thereby become the carriers of the produce of the iflands to

the

the place of its confumption, which will create an interference of foreig. veffels, thereby leffering the number of feamen, and confequently the naval force of the country.

But, if in addition to all that I have already faid, I anfwer, that in return for this accommodation which he may call indulgent, but which I have clearly evinced to be the intereft of Great Britain, confulting the welfare of her iflands, to grant.

I fay, if in return for this accommodation, her fubjects may be admitted to a free ingrefs and egrefs to and from the ports of the United States—What reply will the advocates for this fyftem make?—Whatwil become of Lord Sheffield's reafoning, when weighed in the fcale of comparative proportion? I only wifh them to comprehend the magnitude of the advantage. Men of weak or limited underftandings, will be incapable of extending their ideas, fo as to embrace the vaft field it opens to an enlightened mind.

In the firft place, they will not affuredly deny, that the productions of the United States, to the tranfportation of which, from the propofed arrangement, they are freely to be admitted, will furnifh twice the quantity of bulky materials, that the exports of the Weft Indies do, and will confequently employ twice the quantity of fhipping. —— To ftamp conviction in regard to the truth of this affertion, let them take a view of the rice, indigo, and lumber of Georgia and South Carolina ; — the naval ftores, lumber, and tobacco of North Carolina; — the tobacco wheat, Indian corn, &c. of Virginia and Maryland ; — the flour, lumber corn, and various provifions of Pennfylvania, Delaware, Jerfey and New-York ; —— the fifh, lumber, live flock, &c. of the New England States.

Admit this fact to be afcertained with fatisfactory precifion, will it not be confeffed, that an arrangement, by which both countries are freely admitted to a participation of each other's trade, will be highly advantageous to Great Britain.

This is a pofition, as clear as any mathematical axiom.——Befides, the advantages of Great Britain may be deemed increafing, as the exportation of the bulky produce of the United States, in which her veffels will be employed, will augment, in proportion to the population of the country ;— a population, that will probably be productive beyond all examples of former ages, —— multiplying like the feeds of the harveft.

Whereas, on her part, there is but little room for extenfion of improvement ; — on this point her moft fanguine friends would compound, for her being fixed and ftationary.

But Lord Sheffield argues, that it would be folly to grant the Americans any particular privileges and conceffions, as the treaties with France, and the United Provinces, in direct terms forbid the Britifh being put on a better footing than the inhabitants of thefe countries.

The faculties of this writer muft be ftrangely perverted, — or
his

his defign muft evidently be to delude the public mind, by giving fo falfe a conftruction to this part of the treaties.

Can it be imagined, on the principles of common fenfe, that if the French and Dutch exclude the Americans from a fhare of their Weft India trade, the United States will grant to the inhabitants of thofe countries, the fame free admiffion into their ports, as to thofe of Great Britain, who may permit an unreftrained participation in their commerce ? In every contract, there is a *quid pro quo* —— openly expreffed, or tacitly implied ; — and it is not to be prefum-ed, that the moft favoured nation can require a benefit, without granting a reciprocal return ; —— it is contrary to the avowed policy of nations, which, it is well underftood, is founded on the bread bafis, of intereft and convenience.

The fame reafons will tend to fruftrate the hopes of Ruffia, who cannot, like the United States, give an equitable equivalent to Great Britain, in return for fuch great conceffions.

France has hitherto, invariably, by her own internal refources, fupplied her iflands abundantly, with many of the neceffaries they ftand in need of, and is ftill in a capacity to do the fame.

With refpect to other articles, (the produce of the United States,) that do not interfere with her own exports, fhe has given free admiffion to them all into her Weft India poffeffions ; —— and in order to gain the advantages of the rum trade, which the Britifh hitherto have exclufively propofed, fhe has ceded particu-lar diftricts in her iflands, for the accommodation of the Ameri-cans, who may chufe to erect diftilleries thereon, which, for their great encouragement, are to be exempt from taxes, for a certain number of years. —— The confummate policy of her councils was never more eminently difplayed, than in this mea-fure.

See Proclamation of the General of Martinico, publifhed in the Public Advertifer.

The aftonifhed planter, in viewing the refpective arrangements of the two countries, will wonder where the genius of Britain, fo famed for her commercial knowledge, has retired.

After having already made it appear that it is the intereft of Great Britain (independent of all other confiderations) to adopt the plan of an open communication between the iflands and the United States, and that it is in the power of the latter to grant more than they receive ; —— I will now have recourfe to an argument, that perhaps will have a falutary effect on thofe, who are the moft difficult to be perfuaded ; —— I mean, the relative fituation of the two countries, which makes it the intereft of Great Britain, more than that of any other European power, to be pointedly connected with the American States.

Let a moment's attention be paid to this fubject, and let the in-ference be fairly and difpaffionately drawn.

Great Britain, by the fuperior fkill and induftry of her inhabi-tants

tants, and some adventitious circumstances, has carried many of her manufactures to a degree of perfection and cheapness, which no other country in Europe has arrived at.

Considering the interior state of her population, compared with some of her rival nations, and the very limited extent of her territory, it must be confessed, that a considerable part of her revenues, to support the immense load of debt she has incured, must be drawn from this source ———— from the industry of her people.

The United States at present offer three millions of inhabitants. rapidly increasing in numbers, all of whom consume more or less of British manufactures, —the productions of art and industry, — in return for which, they give the raw materials —— the produce of agriculture, in their native state.

How infatuated must the councils of your country be, which could tend but for a moment, to disturb so beneficial an intercourse; or suspend the sweets of so lucrative a commerce !

The United States have as yet laid no impositions on the importation of British manufactures, that can have any tendency to restrain the consumption of them;—and many reasons of conspicuous weight and importance continually offer, in favour of establishing such duties; — for by operating as a sumptuary law, such a measure would be of considerable service to a young country by repressing the desire of foreign luxuries, which have already been poured into America, in such abundance, that the States begin to suffer, from not having sufficient produce to remit in payment; ———— which turns the balance of trade greatly against them. — Besides, such restrictions wisely imposed, tend to stimulate and encourage a spirit of industry amongst the people, to aim at similar improvements. ———— *December* 16th. 1783.

But should the impolitic conduct of Great Britain precipitate the adoption of this measure by the respective States, where are her growing resources to counteract the effects of this failure of internal industry ? ———— for it is universally agreed, that no country is more dependent on foreign demand, for the superfluous produce of art and industry; ———— and that the luxury and extravagance of her inhabitants, have already advanced to the ultimate point of abuse, and cannot be so increased, as to augment the home consumption, in proportion to the decrease that will take place on a diminution of foreign trade.

What then will become of all those useful hands, that were employedin supplying the great demand ?

Recollect the cries of suffering thousands, at the time of the non-importation agreement ;———— these people, in their own defence, will emigrate to America.

Such a system of conduct persevered in, will operate in favour of the United States, as effectually, as the revocation of the edict of Nantes did in behalf of the protestant countries of Europe — by holding up America, as the most desirable refuge for the property, arts, and manufactures of Great Britain to retire to ; ————

a country

a country, where civil and religious liberty are upheld in all their purity,—— where, by the exertion of a few years of honest industry, an emigrant is morally sure, of being furnished with the means of becoming an independent freeholder ; — a country, that has laid no impolitic restraints on naturalization ;— whose yoke is easy, and whose burthen's light ; and which indulgently holds out its arms for the reception of the weary and heavy laden of all nations ; and which, notwithstanding the attempts of Great Britain to enslave it, would generously offer an asylum for her persecuted sons, who impressed with a sense of gratitude, " may blush " to think their fathers were its foes. "

But Lord Sheffield exultingly advances, that the Americans cannot forego the British manufactures ;——— and that so far from the necessity of courting their custom, not all the interdicts of Congress, and of the several States, during the war, could prevent their consumption.

To deduce important inferences, from such faulty premises, would be " leaning on a broken reed. " There may be at present some partiality in the States, for British manufactures ;——— yet this predilection arises from cradle prejudices, and has greatly decreased during the war ;— and it would be unwise in Great Britain to place any reliance on a continuation of it : — for the manufactures of other countries, if equally good, and afforded cheaper, will, by a continued competition, be eventually preferred ; especially, as there will be a constant succession of emigrants from different parts of Europe, who have no decided preference in favour of the fashion or quality of British manufactures, and who, by mixing with the mass of the people, will gradually effect a change in their taste.— Already do the Americans begin to complain, that the British manufactures are slighted, and inferior in quality to their usual standard ; — and it is well known, that many of the coarse kinds of stuffs, made at Norwich, Coventry, Spitalfields, and other factories, are shamefully deficient in length, whilst the Dutch, Flemish, and French, usually give a generous surplus in their measures.

But if the assertions of Lord Sheffield were founded on truth, what should be the conduct of Great Britain ?

Surely no circumstance can be more favourable to the aggrandizing a nation of industry, than the possession of a foreign trade with a country, which does not supply its own wants, and in which, the consumers of manufactures, that she furnishes, are continually increasing.

Surrounded by rival nations, whose interests are opposed to hers, does she consider the duties that arise out of such a connection ? They should prompt her to facilitate, by every method in her power the means of making remittances, in return for the manufactures she furnished ; not by prohibiting the sale of American vessels which are sent to England for the payment of British debts ; — by opening her ports for the importation of American produce

free

free of duty ; — not by laying such heavy impositions thereon, as to oblige the merchant to seek a more friendly market ? and by cultivating an intercourse, pointedly intimate, with that country ; — for this is the vernal season, when the seeds of future connection and intimacy with America are to be sown and cultivated ;— not by showing evident marks of pleasure and satisfaction at every fabricated account of the distresses of America

It would be unnecessary to follow Lord Sheffield through the tedious detail of articles that he has enumerated, as constituting the wants of the Americans, the greatest part of which, he asserts, they must absolutely procure from England ; — the fallacy of this account can only be discovered by a person who is acquainted with the nature of the American trade, and the relative quality and price of foreign manufactures.

To oppose assertion to assertion, would not be sufficient to operate conviction on the public mind; — but surely, one who can seriously place the articles of silk, laces, and salt, amongst the number of those which Great Britain can enter into competition with other countries in supplying America with, must either be very ignorant of his subject, or extremely partial to his own country.

On a fair and candid consideration of the foregoing reflections, I think you will be persuad'd, that the beautiful prospect that Lord Sheffield has painted to the eyes of his enraptured countrymen, of the increasing consequence of Great Britain, from his pleasing Arcadian plans will without great care taken to prevent it, and by pursuing a system diametrically opposite to what he has formed, disappear, like the dancing vision of a misty evening.

He reasons, as if the trade of America must irresistibly be confined to its former channel ; whereas I can assure him, that freed from the controul of your Navigation Act, and all the fetters of commercial restraint it will expand itself, as far as seas can carry, or winds can waft it.

He forgets the energy of this young Country, that he is devoting to such humiliating restrictions ; ———— he forgets, that it exhibited, whilst in its cradle, such marks of firmness and vigour of constitution, as like young Hercules to crush the serpent, that wantonly attacked it.

He does not recollect, that it is in the power of the United States, if provoked to it, to have recourse. to recrimination and mutually ill offices, and to establish restrictions similar to those Great Britain may impose, which will be relatively far more prejudicial to her trade and commerce.

An impartial dispassionate Englishman, fully weighing the reasons alledged against the adoption of Lord Sheffield's restraining system, and cordially attached to the interest of Great Britain, will deprecate the fatal measure.

An American, in the same temper of mind, looking forward to the future prosperity and power of his country, and contemplating

ing

ing the tendency of this fyftem towards ftrengthening the union of the States, and making it indiffoluble, will not hefitate to acquiefce without a murmur, to the exiftence of thefe reftraining regulations :— the only objections that can arife, will come from thofe, who, too attentive to temporary inconveniences, do not confider and contraft them, with the many advantages their country will eventually derive ;— who do not confider, that the more trade and intercourfe the United States will have with Great Britain, the greater will be the importation of Britifh manufactures, and the more it will tend to impoverifh and weaken them, and in the fame proportion, contribute to her aggrandizement and power.

Harley-Street, Cavendish-Square, December 16th, 1783.

END OF STRICTURES ON COMMERCE.

PREFACE TO MENTOR.

*T*HE *Author feels himself conftrained to beg his readers indulgence, for the hafty manner, which the fcantinefs of his time (not being able to devote but three evenings to it) has obliged him to obferve in preparing the following addrefs. Indeed this confideration, together with the very different avocations in which he is engaged, and the difinclination he has to controverfial writings, would have prevented him from undertaking it, were it not that no one elfe feemed difpofed to do it, and the repeated denials to the importunities of fome friends, made the laft alternative moft difagreeable.*

It has been his ftudy to ftate the thoughts which occurred in fo fhort a time, in as plain and fimple a manner as he could, and not to puzzle his honeft reader with learned form, or to plague him with frequent quotations from the works of the dead, to fhew his own great reading. The cafe being ftated, he fuppofes his reader competent to judge for himfelf, without fearching the records of antiquity for examples of opinion in like cafes.

MENTOR's

MENTOR's REPLY

TO

PHOCION's LETTER.

RAISE a feather in the air, and it will be impoſſible to de-
termine where it ſhall light ſo it is with a newly raiſed political
ſentiment only granting that there are a few intereſted, both for and
againſt it, to give it a circulation.

When the letter of Phocion, firſt made its appearance the doc-
trines contained in it ſtood ſo oppoſed to common underſtanding, that
I was very far from ſuppoſing that any conſequences ariſing from
them, would make a reply to the letter in the ſmalleſt degree ne-
ceſſary ; ſo far from it, I judged a reply would carry with it, the
appearance of wantonly ſeizing an occaſion to introduce the author
upon the ſtage of politics ; but experience has taught me
that paſſion, pomp, and plauſibility, may paſs even upon an enlightened people, for argument and truth.

This author, while he declaims againſt " heated ſpirits," and
" inflammatory " publications, gives us a ſtriking proof that he
has, in an eminent degree, that great diſqualification for a ſtateſman
an uncontroulable warmth of temper. This letter affords us an
inſtance of the frailty of human nature. It gives us the picture of
a ſtrong and tolerably well informed mind, which, perhaps having
been flattered by ſucceſs in the early ſtage of life, has acquired
too much reſpect for its own capacity, too much contempt for
that of others, and too much vanity to conceal theſe effects.

A ſtateſman ſhould be well informed of the nature of that kind
of evidence, which gives political opinion ; he would then ſee
the poſſibilty of others having materials to reaſon from, which the
haſtineſs of his mind may have overlooked. This would teach him
the uſe of holding in decent reſpect the opinion of others, and of
his being a diſpaſſionate enquirer into the means which produced
them, I can ſuppoſe that Phocion believed himſelf poſſeſſed of an
honeſt warmth ; but want of charity and want of modeſty, in one
who offers himſelf for public inſpection, will never fail to raiſe ſome
bile againſt him.

But my buſineſs is with the political part of Phocion's Letter, not
that which paints the author, and I would apologize for ſaying this
much, if I was not ſo ſtrongly courted to it by his illiberality. For
in writing and acting, I would wiſh forever to ſeparate the ſtateſman or politician, and the man.

C

The

The little regard which Phocion had to method in the arrangement of his arguments, muſt be my excuſe for adopting the ſame
plan. I muſt take him where the weight of his arguments ſeem to reſt.

Firſt, then to his conſtruction of the treaty? (which as his pamphlets are in the hands of moſt of the people, I will not trouble them with a long extract of it here) I beg leave to oppoſe to it
the conſtruction in one of the publications, under the ſignature of
Guſtavus, and leave the public to judge which is faireſt.

"In the 6th article of the treaty it is provided, that no one
"ſhall ſuffer in his perſon, liberty, or property, on account of
"the part he may have taken in the war. The 5th article de-
"ſcribes the perſons provided for, and diſtinguiſhes them into
"three claſſes: Firſt, thoſe that are real Britiſh ſubjects. The
"ſecond, thoſe that were within their lines, and had not taken
"arms againſt the country. The third claſs are deſcribed by
"the proviſion that is made for them, viz. They ſhall have
"liberty to go into any part of the United States, for twelve
"months, to ſolicit a reſtoration of their eſtates that may have
"been confiſcated. This claſs muſt be thoſe, who, belonging to
"America, have taken arms againſt their country. The firſt and
"ſecond claſs, it is agreed, that Congreſs ſhall *recommend* to the
"ſtates, a reſtoration of their property. The third it ſeems were
"too infamous for the Engliſh miniſter to aſk any conſideration for,
"except the wretched privilege of aſking it for themſelves. But
"I can find no where, even a requeſt, and that only implied, that
"any of the three claſſes may dwell among us, and enjoy the im-
"munities and privileges of citizens; for the firſt claſs are confi-
"dered as former ſubjects, the ſecond and third as acquired
"ſubjects of England."

But Phocion ſtarts another difficulty: He ſays, to imagine, that
by eſpouſing the cauſe of Great Britain, they become aliens, is to
admit, that ſubjects may, at pleaſure, renounce their allegiance
to the ſtate of which they were members, and devote themſelves
to a foreign juriſdiction; "a principle," he adds, "contrary
to law, and ſubverſive of government."

To this I reply, that if there was nothing more in the caſe than
their adhering to the then enemies of our country, I would readily
join Phocion in opinion, that this action ſimply, ſhould not be
conſtrued to amount to alienation; but it ſhould be conſtrued to
amount to treaſon. So, inſtead of aliens, I would render them
traitors, and as ſuch, put the penal laws in force againſt them.

But it is by treaty, that they become aliens or ſubjects of England. By the treaty England adopted them as ſubjects, and by
ratifying that treaty, the ſtates, and this ſtate, from the ſhare
ſhe had in it, conſented to that adoption. And this is the great
benefit of the treaty to them, which Phocion ſays, we would violate; whereas it appears that we, who he dubs heated and
deſigning men, are the real ſupporters of it,

Granting

Granting them to be aliens, Phocion continues, they cannot hold real property under our government, their real estates then must be considered as belonging to the public, this is confiscation, and thereby the treaty is violated. I answer, that they are aliens, but aliens stipulated for. If in doing this, our ministers have exceeded the powers given them, and Congress also, by acceding to what they have done ; or, if they agreed to an article in the treaty, which wars with the nature of government or with the particular genius of ours, let it be so declared, and also the consequence of the blunder ; then we may take up the subject in another point of view. But till then we must consider it as it is, and take it for granted that it is right.

But for my own part, I cannot see the inconsistency of it. Suppose the British East India company had claims to certain lands in America, before her separation from England, and by an article of the treaty it should be agreed, that they should have the privilege of selling it, some might doubt the justice of it, but I think none could doubt the right.

To make it appear, that in removing a number of these people, prosecutions of some kind or other would be necessary, and which are forbid by the treaty, seems to be a chief design of Phocion. Beside others which have been observed, he starts this : How will it be determined, but by prosecution, who have so adhered to the enemy, as in a legal sense to amount to a crime ? I answer, in the first place, that no question of law arises on the subject.

It is by treaty, and not by law, that we are to judge of them ; for the ratification of that has, in effect, repealed all the laws that stood in force against them. If the treaty have not this power, then have we played the cheat, not only with England, but with every power that was represented in that Congress, which settled the terms of peace. In the second place, that the treaty itself makes the distinction that otherwise would be wanting ; and all that is necessary for the legislature in this particular is, by an act of grace to make a distinction of a very different kind ; to distinguish and restore to citizenship, the deserving of those who are by treaty made subjects of England.

I presume it must by this time clearly appear, that the people we are speaking of are the subjects of England. It then remains to see, what necessity demands, and what justice and honour will allow to be done with them ; and in this investigation, let us throw aside every passion, but that which is concerned for the safety and true interest of the state.

Before I proceed, permit me to lay it down, as a maxim, that it is a principle coincident with the very nature of society, that there be a power vested in it, in some form or other, adequate to the purpose, not only of correcting any present evil in it, but to prevent a probable future one.

Though

Though I abhor all reasonings which tend to make less heinous the dreadful sin of taking arms against our country, both as it regards the eternal law of justice, and also good policy ; yet as the country has agreed by a solemn compact, not to take vengeance of those of this character in America, both our honour and interest are concerned to preserve this compact inviolate, so upon this occasion I shall dismiss all that passion arising from a lively recollection of what this country has sustained from them, would dictate, and speak of them only as they respect our political safety, as a morbid humour in our political body, which requires healthy remedies to expel.

After a farmer has prepared his ground, would he mix cockle with his seed-wheat to grow up with, and contaminate the wholesome grain ? In establishing a young empire, should we leave the principle of sedition in its foundation ? But Phocion will tell us that this is a bug-bear danger. *Make it their interest and they will be good subjects.* God forbid, the government should make it their interest to be its friends ; for to do this, would be to bring the principles of the government to suit *them*, not them to suit *it*. The tory principle, where it has been long entertained, and where it has long beat unison with the passions, is more fixed and immoveable than the best established government   I speak of those who have been much concerned in government speculation. Of political opinions, those which respect monarchical and republican governments, are most opposed of course most irreconcileable ; they beget a contempt for each other, in the members of the two governments.

To show that our fears for the well-being of our government on this occasion, are founded in reason, and not ideal, beside what has been already said, let us consider the number and quality of the people, who, I am ashamed to say, are the subjects of dispute, and the difference between the government which their principles contend for, and ours.

In a monarchical government, I grant the doctrine of Phocion may obtain. There fear might make it their interest to be good subjects ; the fear of offending against the government. But, in a republican government, the people are their own governors. A republican government must take its shape from the opinion of the people, and is variable, as the opinions of its component parts may vary ; hence the necessity of correcting that evil, which may spring from a corruption of opinion, and though it may be confined to a few at first, it may communicate to the overturning of the government. The number of those who are in reality malcontents in America, are not so small as may be imagined ; nor are their views and hopes so humble as many suppose.

I have said that government has a right to anticipate probable evils. The tory principle contains in it a mortal and irreconcileable hatred to our government. That this principle will be communicated, is too probable, when we consider the wealth,
                                                              the

the art, the perseverance and fashion of many of its present posses-
sors.

On the other hand, let us consider the indigence which the ra-
vages of a long and accursed war have created in the other party,
which must cause them assiduously to attend to their own private concerns. For though some of them still preserve a lively attention
to the government, yet in many the effect which I have mentioned, has been wrought; and in a little time the last spasms of the
republican spirit will be over, the meager ghost of poverty with
all her train of evils, being constantly before them, every other
consideration will yield to the spur of necessity. In the mean
while, the mal-contents are left with the means, and can afford
the leisure to get into administration. This, fellow citizens is the
condition of affairs; ——— I blush to proclaim it, to which the
writings and sayings of whigs tend to bring you! ——— For Phocion
tells you, that he has been an eminent servant of the republic in
establishing her independency. If a revolution is effected in the
manner above stated, however infamous the means, yet when the
revolution is completed, it is a just one, because it must be sup-
posed that a majority of opinions are for it. Therefore I say, it
is importantly the duty of the present government to anticipate
such an evil, by removing the causes of pravity of opinion. But
short of a revolution, a perversion of the principles of our government, which is more easily wrought, may be as wounding to the
upright republican.

With regard to England's renewing her claim to the country,
on the supposition that ill policy abroad, and anarchy at home,
should invite her to it, I am clearly of opinion it would not be her
interest to do it; for, if she should succeed, the extent and rapid
growth of the country would prevent its being long tributary to
that distant island. I am also fully convinced, that the late and
present ministry of England did not, and do not, wish for the
re-union of the country upon any other terms than as a farm,
from which she is to derive *substantial revenue*, without allowing
the tenant any vote in the disposition of it. But we are not to
calculate what is only the real interest of a nation, whose monarch
has the right of making peace and war. Suppose the inclination
of the present king should not lead him to reclaim the country;
yet, his son, when he comes to the throne, may be ambitious for
the glory of recovering the lost dominion of his father. And as to
the difficulty of obtaining money from parliament to carry on an
unreasonable war, the rapid corruption of that people will probably soon remove it.

There is no other way of preventing this probable corruption
of opinion, but by removing the cause, which I have asserted to
be the mal-contents of America. Having, as we presume, shewn
the necessity, let us now, as proposed, enquire if honour and
equity will consent to the measure.

The treaty which justice and honour forbid us to violate, does

not

not, even upon fo liberal a conftruction, as I believe Phocion himfelf would give it, debar the ftates from making laws that may
be falutary to the government, and advantageous to the people,
though in their confequences they may operate againft the intereft
of the fubjects of England. Suppofe a line to be drawn, and
the deferving of thofe, who by treaty are made fubjects of
England, fhould be re-adopted, and invefted with all the privileges of citizens; and, after this, laws fhould be paffed, giving the citizens the exclufive benefits of trade. This law would
operate no more againft the fubjects of England that are here, than
againft thofe who are at home, except in this, the effect of the
law in one cafe, fends thefe home, and in the other cafe, keeps
them there, or rather prevents their coming here as traders.

There was a time when the people of England confidered themfelves in danger from a corruption of opinion of another kind — I
mean of religious opinion. Few proteftants complained of it as
unjuft or difhonourable, that the government enacted laws to fup-
prefs the growth of the Roman Catholic religion.

A government has a clearer right to interfere in checking the
promulgation of depravity in political, than in religious opinion.
If the tory principle fhould be repreffed in this way, it is a remedy
ufed for the health and prefervation of the body politic, and as
fuch no one, not even the tories, can complain of it as unjuft,
though they may deprecate the hardfhip of the meafure as applied
to themfelves.

In the firft cafe, that is againft laws for exclufive trade, it has
been objected, that by removing thefe people we remove a great
part of the filver, and gold out of the ftate. With as much pro-
priety it may be argued againft the meafure, that we fhould remove
a great part of the writing paper out of the ftate.

Money is a conveniency, not an article of trade; being fuch,
wherever trade centers money will. The importance of this city,
as a place of trade, is not owing to the quantity of money that is
now in it, or that ever was in it, at any one time. It is with effects
that we trade, and the mercantile confequence of this town arifes
from its being central to the effects of this and the adjoining ftates,
and the conveniency of its water communication. Suppofe this
city traded only with the effects of this ftate, then its quantity of
trade would be in exact proportion to the annual produce of the
ftate, though there fhould not be an ounce of filver or gold in the
place to-morrow.

Another objection ftill more futile has been made againft a law for
exclufive trade. That we prevent the merchants of England from
coming over and fettling with us, and their fhips from vifiting us,
which would be a dreadful misfortune to the trading intereft of the
ftate. " Open your arms, or ports," (I do not remember which)
faid the writer of a hand bill, " to the fhips of foreign nations."

Unlefs Congrefs fhould have in contemplation to give fome particular privileges to the French nation, and to which I fhall have no
objection,

obj .tion, I declare I have not a wish ever to see a foreign vessel, or a foreign merchant, visit this continent, except as a traveller. I would not be understood to wish a prohibition of foreign vessels to our harbours ; but I wish they may be discouraged, by encouraging ship-building here. With us, who have it in our power to make vessels and naval stores, articles of export ; and who want articles of export so much, would it be to our interest to carry on our trade in foreign bottoms ? —— With regard to foreign merchants, it is well known that there are, at present, more adventurers in trade, in America, than there is trade to support, *that is*, the spirit of trade is more than in proportion to its quantity. When foreign merchants migrate to the two Americas, it is generally with a view to mend or make their fortunes, and to return home and enjoy them. Can such men feel themselves interested in the welfare of our government ? Is it not more probable that they will still consider themselves of the nation which they left ; and as far as they have influence in the government, use it for the interest of their own nation, to which they still feel themselves belonging ? Would it then be so essentially our duty to encourage such settlers to supplant our own traders ; and who, if they acquire fortunes, is it probable they will be used to the benefit of our government?

There is a kind of settlers that I could wish might be encouraged from all countries ; these are husbandmen and manufacturers. When these migrate, they do it with a view to remain where they settle. Beside these, scientific men of all kinds should be encouraged to visit us. For, whether they become permanent residents or not, they are useful while they do stay.

I would encourage husbandmen and manufacturers to come to the country, and discourage traders, for the same reason that I would encourage articles of export, and discourage articles of import, by holding out bounties on the one side, and imposts on the other.

So general is the cry of the balance of trade being against America, that the blockhead who wants skill to balance his cane, will put on the face of business, and tell me, " the balance of trade is against us." Will importing foreign merchants into the country tend to place this balance in its favour. The truth is, a balance of trade cannot exist against a country longer than a year or two, For if the imports of this year exceed the exports, the balance must be paid the next year. If the articles of export should not be so increased, as by the next year to make up the balance, then the articles of import will be proportionably diminished. A balance cannot be always due. The imports and exports must, in the long run, bear an exact proportion to each other. If our exports are small, our imports must consequently be small. The nation then cannot abound in foreign productions ; they cannot be in a state of affluence,

This teaches us a plain and simple truth, viz. That the riches of a nation are derived from the cultivation of its land, and its
manufactures

manufacturies. Merchants are the agents of the farmers and manufacturers, to exchange their commodities for those of other countries, which this will not produce.

This is a simple state of the case; I wish I had leisure to enter more fully into it.

To increase the wealth of our state then, we should invite husbandmen and manufacturers into the country, and look coldly on traders, for that part of our community is already too numerous, and will probably cause the temporary inconvenience which I have mentioned, of placing the balance of trade against us for a time, which must create a scarcity of foreign commodities for some time after. Unless greater exertions in cultivating the land should immediately succeed it and make up the balance.

Phocion's letter being essentially, though not minutely answered, some of his arguments which are not noticed, depending upon principles which have been disproved, some not applying at all to the case in question, and some in reality unexceptionable, I will take leave of my reader, after observing, that I do not wish the policy of the state to take into consideration the small sinner from the ignorant. Our government is in no danger: It is the bell-weathers of the flock that we should guard against.

There is no form of government so delicate in its nature, and which requires so much attention to preserve, as that which exists in the minds of the people. While corruption is kept out of it, there is no form of government so honourable to men, and so happy to the partaker of it; and when corrupted, there is no government so much to be detested and avoided. Considering things in this point of view, and considering what it has cost us to establish this government, what it would have cost us if we had failed in it, I am not willing to trifle with the acquisition. To risque it from a false notion of generosity, or because it is easy for Phocion and others to bestow the epithet of vindictive on the salutary measures that may be proposed for its preservation.

We did at the commencement of the war, and have in the whole course of it, kept it in view as a debt which we owed to posterity, to bequeath to them that liberty which we recived from our ancestors. Having got this in our power by an hazardous and dreadful conflict, to suffer the inestimable acquisition to perish by neglect, would be not only to betray them but ourselves.

THE   END   OF   MENTOR's   REPLY.

Philadelphia March 30th. 1784

MEMORANDUM. *Every Gentleman that has been supplied with these two Pamphlets in their present imperfect situation, are requested to be so very obliging as to call for their completion at* BELL's BOOK-STORE, *near St. Paul's Church, in Third-Street, as soon as they are Advertised, and the favour will be gratefully acknowledged, By their respectful Servant,*

ROBERT BELL.